Dec '95

FAMINE

DESMOND EGAN BOOKS

POETRY
  Midland 1972
  Leaves 1974
  Siege! 1977
  Woodcutter 1978
  Athlone? 1980
  Seeing Double 1983
  Snapdragon 1983 1991
  Poems for Peace 1986
  A Song for my Father 1989
  Peninsula 1992
  In the Holocaust of Autumn 1994
  Poems for Eimear 1994
  Famine 1997

COLLECTIONS
  Collected Poems 1983 1984
  Selected Poems (Editor Hugh Kenner) 1992
  Elegies (1972-1996) 1996

PROSE
  The Death of Metaphor Selected Prose 1990 1991

TRANSLATIONS
  Euripides, Medea 1991 1997
  Sophocles, Philoctetes 1997

IN TRANSLATION
  Terre et Paix (French/English) 1988
  Echobogen (Dutch/English) 1990
  Quel Sole Storno Che Gelido Passa (Italian/English) 1992
  Gedichte (German/English) 1994
  Un Poeta d'Irlanda (Italian/English) 1995
  Paper Cranes (Japanese/English) 1995
  Peninsula (French/English) 1996
  Poesie Scelte (Italian/English) 1997
  Have Mercy on the Poet (Czech/ English) 1997

CRITICAL STUDIES
  Desmond Egan: The Poet and His Work
    edited by Hugh Kenner USA 1990
  Desmond Egan: A Critical Study
    Brian Arkins USA 1992

DESMOND EGAN
famine

with drawings by James McKenna

Ireland
1997

GOLDSMITH

First published in 1997 by
THE GOLDSMITH PRESS LTD
Newbridge
Co Kildare
Ireland

Copyright © Desmond Egan 1997

Illustrations © James McKenna 1997
Back cover portrait © Wilhelm Föckersperger 1997

ISBN: 1 8769481 42 4

The right of Desmond Egan to be identified as author of this work has been asserted by him in accordance with the Copyright, Design and Patents Act 1988.

Typesetting: Bernadette Smyth
Colour Separations: Gerry Breen, IrishLitho Print
Printed by: Tully Print, Kildare

ACKNOWLEDGMENTS

Four of these poems appraised in a limited edition, published by Milestone Press, USA 1996

Special thanks to James McKenna for permission to reproduce his wood sculpture
   Famine Spectre: The Corn Goddess Intervenes
(walnut; height 8.5 feet) which was first exhibited at the Gerard Manley Hopkins International Summer School 1996; and for the drawings which he made for this book.

Thanks also to Wilhelm Föckersperger for the back cover portrait.

CONTENTS

Famine   a sequence

		page
I	the stink of famine	15
II	from as far away as Arkansas	17
III	save one person save a world yes	19
IV	between the planks and the backword waves	21
V	took away our great forests	25
VI	a tin whistle dances between decks	27
VII	famine of feeling	29
VIII	and how could nature our relation	31
IX	but the kenosis too	35
X	paddleboats lighting passages	37
XI	EPILOGUE	39

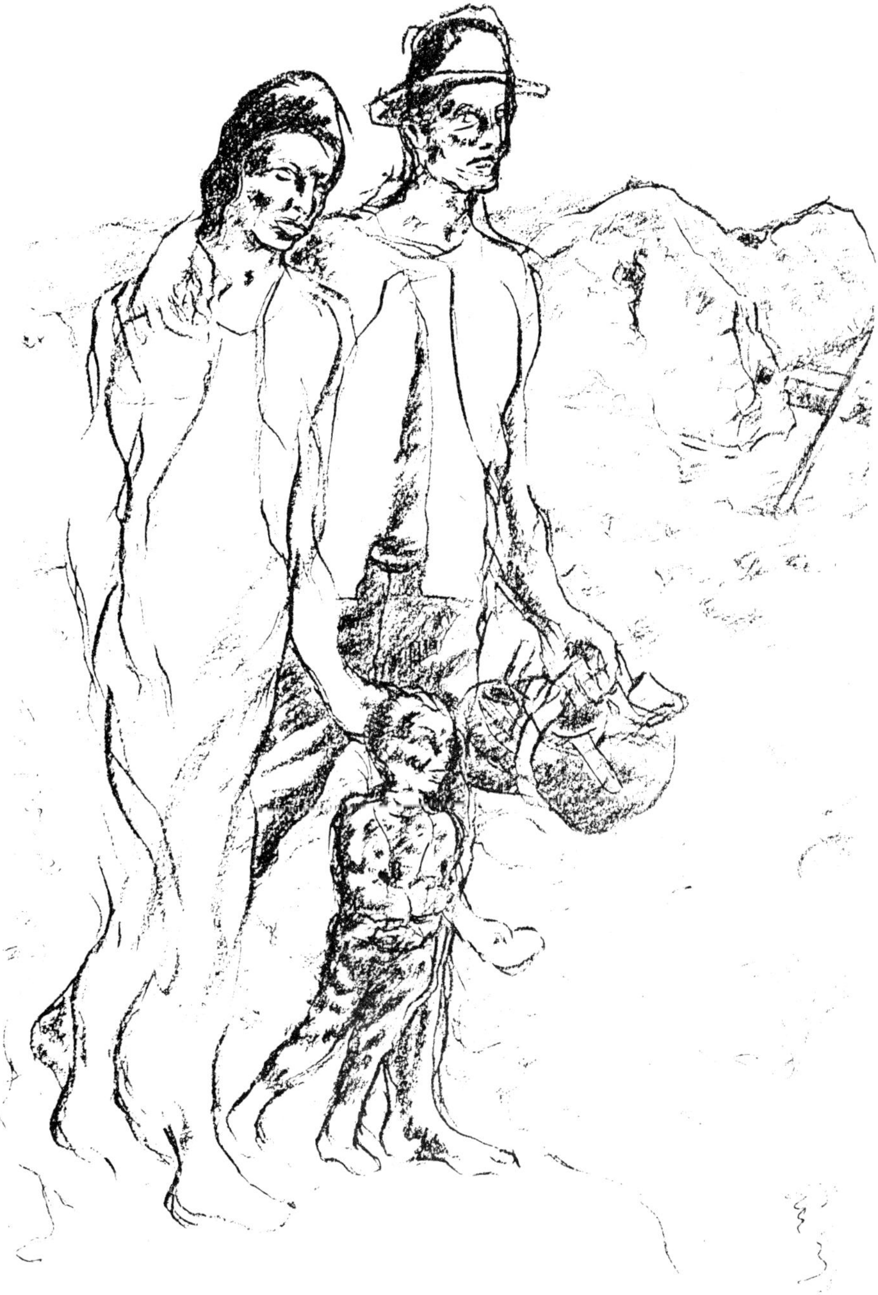

For James McKenna
óir ní bheidh a leithéid ann arís

FAMINE a sequence

I

the stink of famine
hangs in the bushes still
in the sad celtic hedges

you can catch it
down the lines of our landscape
get its taste on every meal

listen
there is famine in our music

famine behind our faces

it is only a field away
has made us all immigrants
guilty for having survived

has separated us from language
cut us from our culture
built blocks around belief

left us on our own

>

ashamed to be seen
walking out beauty so
honoured by our ancestors

but fostered now to peasants
the drivers of motorway diggers
unearthing bones by accident
under the disappearing hills

II

from as far away as Arkansas
they could hear the children

more clearly than their masters could
next door in landlord London where
mostly they lurked on the edges as
sack drinkers ballers the semi sophisticates
starving at heart
the condition of their absentee tenants
metaphor enough

and for the politicians too
who wanted power but didn't know why
their motto *laissez mourirr* if such
were the holy will of trade

a century and a half later
you can catch that weeping

of boys and girls forced to miss
life as well as school
while the youngsters they loved
half naked creatures
slowly bloated with death

even the towns were abandoned
to knots of unspeaking labourers

\>

no one wanting to say *famine*
not even to the hinged
coffin at the workhouse

and the destitute went home
to the hovels of whimpering

so much grief cannot be buried down the fields
or under tumbled cabins those common
monuments to a great race
that never learned to beg

which saved all Europe

III

save one person save a world yes
but kill one and
something goes out of everything

that is why we who lost
the provinces of hope
who had our own holocaust in
medieval 1847

all the centuries of exile
in our own country
massacres too many to mention
carry a sadness in the blood
a walk a look an acent
some bitter rhythm a wounded shadow
wear like the Jews
humour as a vest

sensing that each of us has lost
part of what we should have been

IV

between the planks and the
backward waves
another hunger begins

as the dear gaunt faces drop
behind with their language

people whose humour alone
could
stab at a lonely mind unused
to strangers

like a flash of the stonewall
plot
with potatoes a few flowers
and sunlight cornered as if
everything were just perfect

the bridge too its footpath
learned by heart
the water that never got tired
those ditches of the only
known extravagance

>

the greatest blessing
ask the natives

children should be taught
pride in
their imperial heritage its
transformation of the
world
for the lasting benefit of
literally millions

time we gave serious
thought to
the nobler instincts that
drove
generations of Britons
to risk their lives building
The Empire

to make a profit
under God

a voice from the village morning
singing across years and countries *the locals are what*
of what might have been *would be understood*
in England as starved
and what is understood
the girl with the eyes *in Ireland as halfstarved*
engaged to landlord death

and the bluebottle quiet in which
a nextdoor neighbour whose ancestors
had taught him nothing about begging was
lying on his face like a rabbit

memory is the first exile

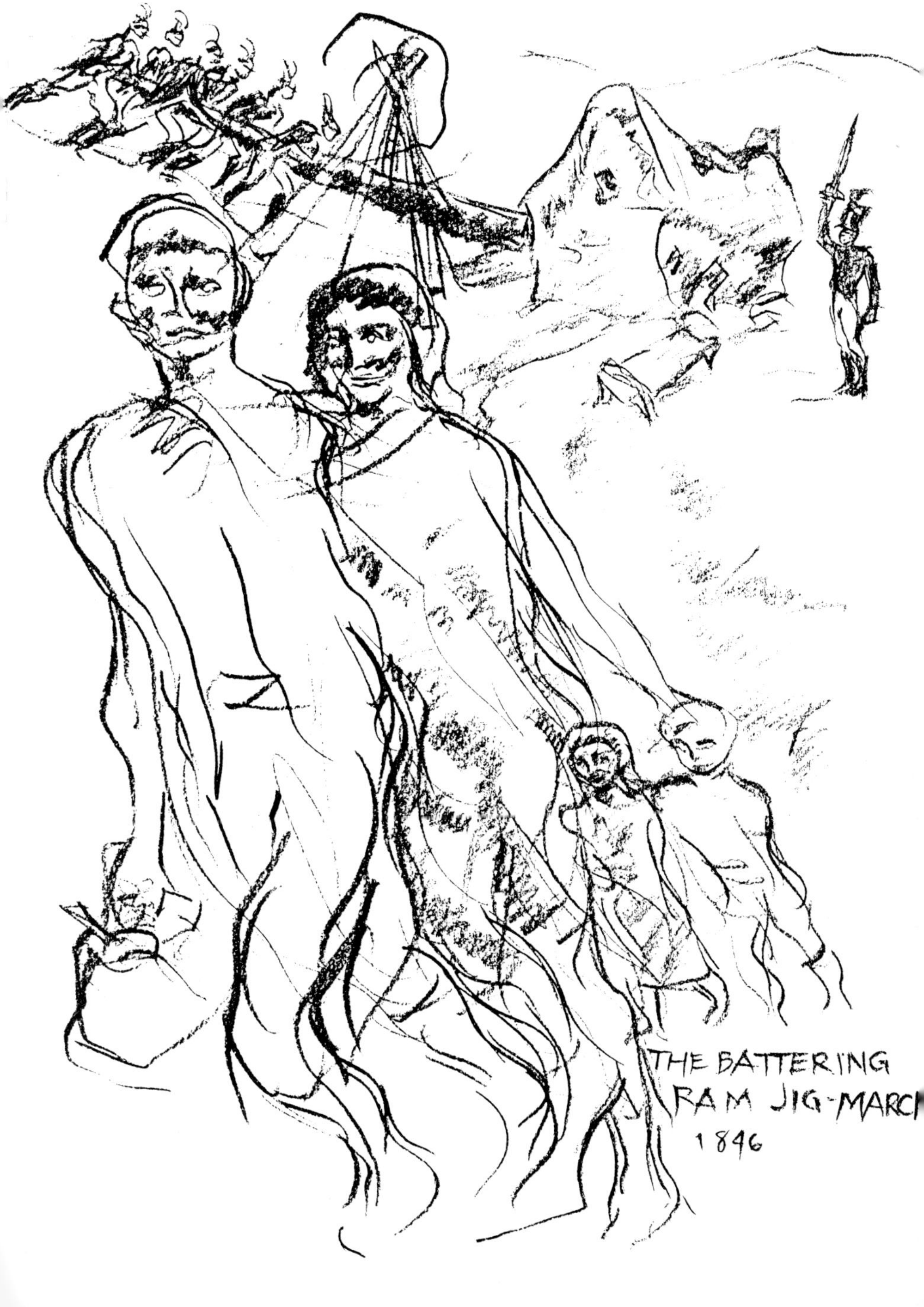
THE BATTERING
RAM JIG-MARC
1846

V

took away our great forests
took our cattle away
took away our farming
our wool our linen our glass
grabbed the very plots
from under our hungry eyes
starved our language
tried our religion too
tumbled a nation's destiny
    drove us
into the ditches of Europe
and onto the sad tides

one thousand years of murder
one thousand years of plunder
one thousand years of rape
the curse of Raleigh on you
the curse of Cromwell too
one thousand years in cells
one thousand years climbing
the gallows the gibbet the wooden triangle
and the disciplined army lash
beginning at 500 strokes

                                 >

the greatest blessing
ask the natives

children should be taught
    pride in
their imperial heritage its
transformation of the
    world
for the lasting benefit of
literally millions

time we gave serious
    thought to
the nobler instincts that
    drove
generations of Britons
to risk their lives building
The Empire

to make a profit
under God

the locals are what would
    be understood
in England as starved
and what is understood
in Ireland as half-starved

one thousand years
one thousand years
of war and famine and plague
one thousand years on the run

one thousand years of dying
instead of being alive

took away our childhood
took our parents away
sisters brothers families
took away our heroes
too bitter too bitter a list
knotted our future into a past
to whip us with

gave us pax Britannica
slavery beneath the slavery
of the slaving capital of the world
gave us plenty to die for

gave us their neuroses
the nervous tics of empire
their need to be admired

and threw in as a bonus
their honest astonishment at
our refusal to be improved

VI

a tin whistle dances between decks
on one of the rat ships
smoking towards Liverpool

and this spirit tune will soon
move between the barges the lights
    the warehouses
to where the *Ticonderoga* the*Chasca*
the *Loodaniah* lie at anchor
within a new contagion of
slums runners crimps renters bosses

to queue up eventually
on one more gangway
out onto the permanent swell
the long long goodbye
lingering into a life

dull canvases on such a wide horizon
and white Irish faces turning
back like Colmcille

over waves that have no memories

try try to be tough

remember the scene
    you left

there's no returning
no matter what

you're one of
the
lucky
ones

and the years
turn into feelings

VII

famine of feeling
famine of words
famine of the space
of fields
of beauty
of days

of any past or present

famine famine of everything

under that starvation
what chance is there for high crosses

for our brief poetry

VIII

and how could nature our relation   *they utter no complaint*
remain untouched by such starvation by
the lives which flitted like leaves   *they do not beg*
about our island graveyard?

but
follow
you can come across it still   *around*

in
in the weals across a hillscape   *silent*
in the violence of bushes   *crowds*
in the dead stones of a cabin wall
holding their story under galvanise

in the bare cholera fields

sometimes you can surprise it
in the deeper dark within a hedge
in the bitter twist of an old oak
or a river's slide into sadness

hear it down the empty woods

in the silence of birds wheeling

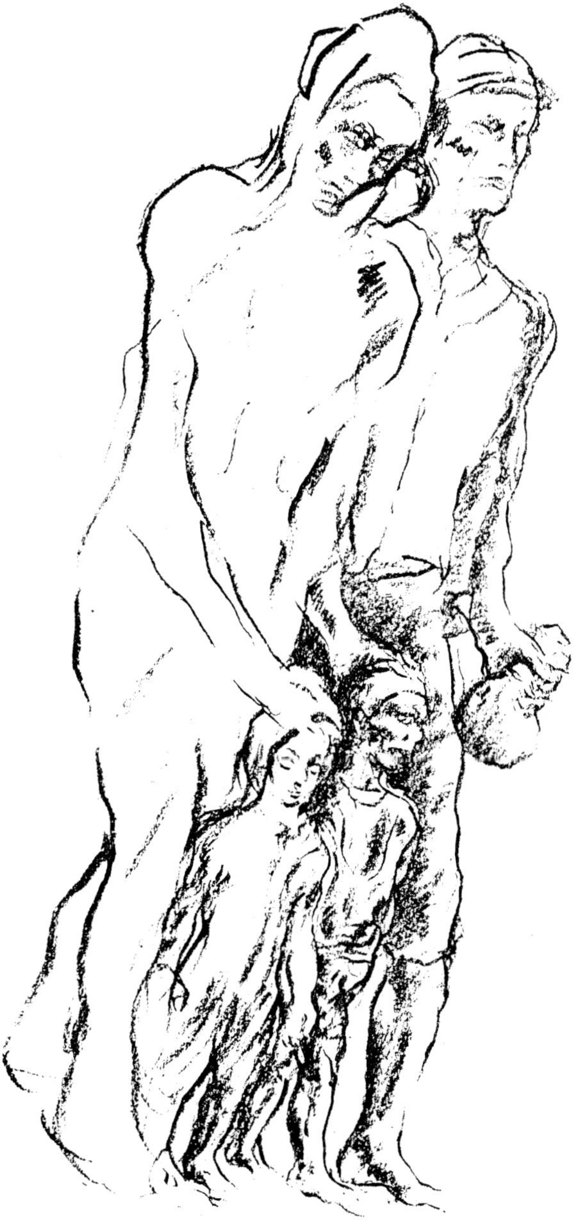

IX

but the *kenosis* too remember

that gradual shedding of
the gravity of living
a dropping as of worn clothes
of all that dies

and down the final simple hours
that floating closer to otherness
when with mystical eyes
of a water clearness
the spirit shyly peeps through those
last tatters of being

when a look becomes a legacy

to carry across time and the world

X

paddleboats lighting passages
up the Mississippi
and the other ways to elsewhere

to Little Rock and states
with names like dark faces

Refugio beyond New Orleans
Baton Rouge Fort Smith
and after black Arkansas
Memphis
St. Louis
Iowa
and New Wexford already waiting
for those who could make it

into riverways broader than the Shannon
they steam along without a present
immigrants stripped to their ancestors

that Celtic lightness

EPILOGUE

and that black disease
is active still

a miasma over our South
over sad Dublin

over Divis St. Flats
over The Bogside
over Portstewart-by-the-Sea

how long Lord?

Lord how long?